Insect Homes

THERESE HOPKINS

PowerKiDS
press™
New York

Published in 2009 by The Rosen Publishing Group, Inc.
29 East 21st Street, New York, NY 10010

First Edition

Editor: Nicole Pristash
Book Design: Kate Laczynski
Photo Researcher: Jessica Gerweck

Photo Credits: Cover, pp. 1, 5, 7, 9, 13, 15, 17, 19, 23, 24 (insects), 24 (mound), 24 (termites), 24 (wasps) Shutterstock.com; pp. 11, 24 (tunnels) © Mark Moffett/Getty Images; p. 21 © Ben Van Den Brink/Foto Natura/Getty Images.

Library of Congress Cataloging-in-Publication Data

Hopkins, Therese.
  Insect homes / Therese Hopkins. — 1st ed.
      p. cm. — (Home sweet home)
  Includes index.
  ISBN 978-1-4358-2695-3 (library binding) — ISBN 978-1-4358-3069-1 (pbk.)
ISBN 978-1-4358-3081-3 (6-pack)
  1. Insects—Habitations—Juvenile literature. I. Title.
  QL467.2.H665 2009
  595.7156′4—dc22
                                    2008022055

Manufactured in the United States of America

CONTENTS

Some **insects** build homes where they live together in a large group. This is a nest in which **wasps** live.

5

This wasp is building a nest in a tree. The queen wasp will lay her eggs in this nest.

Termites eat dirt and wood, so they live underground and inside trees.

Inside their homes, termites build long **tunnels** to live in and to keep their eggs safe.

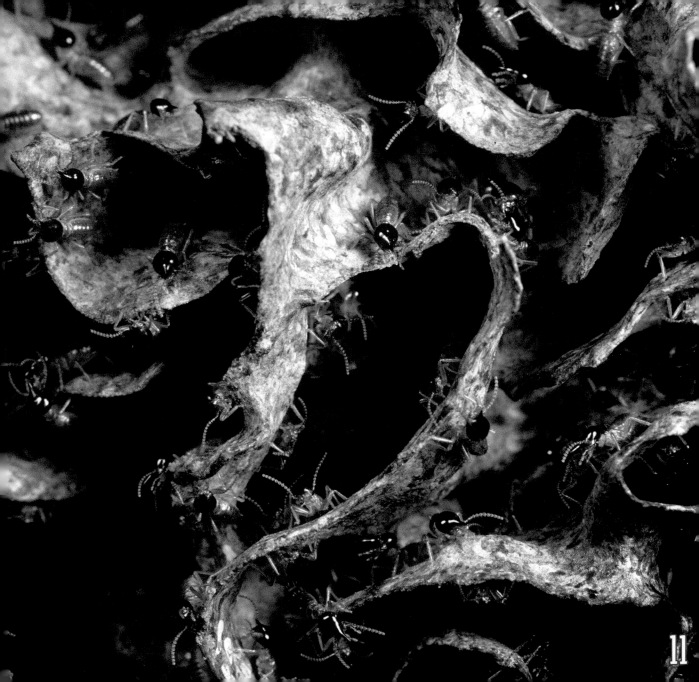
11

A termite **mound** is made when a termite nest grows above the ground.

13

The ant is another insect that builds tunnels underground.

When ants dig a tunnel,
they pile the dirt outside.
This makes an anthill.

These worker ants are taking care of their eggs and their young inside the nest.

Honeybees build their homes in trees. Honeybee homes are called hives.

Honeybees store eggs and honey inside their hive.

23

WORDS TO KNOW

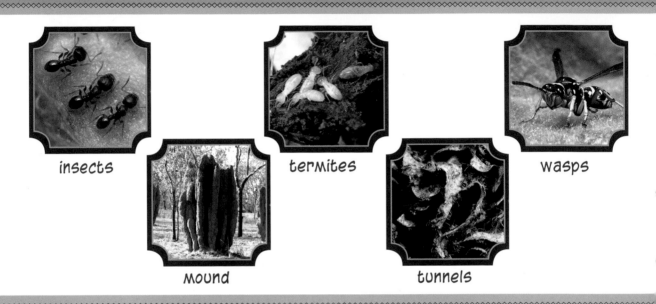

insects

termites

wasps

mound

tunnels

WEB SITES

Due to the changing nature of Internet links, PowerKids Press has developed an online list of Web sites related to the subject of this book. This site is updated regularly. Please use this link to access the list:
www.powerkidslinks.com/hsh/insect/